POEMS
for the
Very Young

KINGFISHER
a Houghton Mifflin Company imprint
222 Berkeley Street
Boston, Massachusetts 02116
www.houghtonmifflinbooks.com

First published in hardcover in 1993
First published in paperback in 1996
First published in this format in 2004

10 9 8 7 6 5 4 3

LIBRARY OF CONGRESS CATALOGING-IN-PUBLICATION DATA
Poems for the very young/compiled by Michael Rosen:
illustrated by
Bob Graham.—1st American ed.
p. cm.
Includes index.
Summary: An illustrated collection of modern and
traditional poems
by a variety of authors from different parts of the world.
1. Children's poetry, English. [1. Poetry—Collections.]
I. Rosen, Michael. II. Graham, Bob ill.
III. Title
PR1175.3.P565 1993
821.008'09282—dc20 92–45574 CIP AC

ISBN 0-7534-5816-0

Printed in China
3TR/0904/TIMS/PW(MA)/128MA

POEMS
for the
Very Young

Selected by
Michael Rosen

Illustrated by
Bob Graham

KINGFISHER
BOSTON

Just for Jack
B.G.

INTRODUCTION

Whenen I go to France, I can understand a lot of what people are saying, but not everything. What I don't understand, I hear as sounds, rhythms, and tones — the physical side of language. I am, then, more aware, more in touch with the physical. Very young children are, I think, in a similar situation and we can often hear them playing with the sounds of language.

Of all the ways of using words, poetry is surely the most physical and is a particularly appropriate kind of literature to give to children. So the core of this collection is a playful use of words and sounds.

But play is not an end in itself; it is a means to discovering and understanding the way things work, the way we are. So here also are ideas, feelings, and observations chosen for their tone of discovery and revelation.

For the book to work, for it to happen, it needs readers: little and big people to run their fingers over the pages, pore over Bob Graham's witty and life-full pictures, and to sing, shout, whisper, chant, and sigh the words any time of day or night. As I learnt to say from American writers — Enjoy!

Michael Rosen

WAKEY, WAKEY

Wakey, wakey, rise and shine,
Make your bed,
And then make mine.

ANON

THE DUSTMAN

Every Thursday morning,
Before you're quite awake,
Without the slightest warning
The house begins to shake
With a Biff!...Bang!
Biff! Bang! Bash!

It's the dustman, who begins
(Bang!...Crash!)
To empty both the bins
Of their rubbish and their ash,
With a Biff!...Bang!
Biff! Bang! Bash!

CLIVE SANSOM

I can put my socks on,
I can find my vest,
I can put my pants on —
I can't do the rest.

TONY BRADMAN

HAIR

I despair
About hair
    With all the fuss
    For us
Of snipping
And clipping,
    Of curling
    And twirling,
Of tying
And drying,
    And lopping
    And flopping,
And flurries
And worries,
    About strength,
    The length,
As it nears
The ears
    Or shoulder.
    When you're older
It turns gray
Or goes away
    Or leaves a fuzz
    Hair does!

MAX FATCHEN

BUTTONS

Buttons, buttons,
I can do up buttons!
I do all my buttons up
When I go to town.
For I have six buttons,
Big round buttons,
Six buttons on my coat
All colored brown!

W. KINGDON-WARD

9

UP TO THE CEILING

Daddy lifts me
up to the ceiling.
Daddy swings me
down to the floor.
Daddy! Daddy!
More! More! MORE!
Up to the ceiling,
down to the floor.

CHARLES THOMSON

TO MARKET, TO MARKET

To market, to market, to buy a plum cake,
Back again, back again, baby is late;
To market, to market, to buy a plum bun,
Back again, back again, market is done.

ANON

SUGARCAKE BUBBLE

Sugarcake, Sugarcake
    Bubbling in a pot
Bubble, Bubble Sugarcake
    Bubble thick and hot

Sugarcake, Sugarcake
    Spice and coconut
Sweet and sticky
    Brown and gooey

I could eat the lot.

GRACE NICHOLS

One, two, three, four,
Mary at the cottage door,
Eating cherries off a plate,
Five, six, seven, eight.

ANON

When Jacky's a good boy,
    He shall have cakes and custard;
But when he does nothing but cry,
    He shall have nothing but mustard.

ANON

11

THE BARBER

Tiddly Wink the barber
Went to shave his father
Soap slip
Cut lip
Tiddly Wink the barber.

ANON

THE WINDOW CLEANER

When I grow up I want to be
A window cleaning man
And make the windows in our street
As shiny as I can.
I'll put my ladder by the wall
And up the steps I'll go
But when I'm up there with my pail
I hope the wind won't blow.

M. LONG

MRS. PECK-PIGEON

Mrs. Peck-Pigeon
Is picking for bread,
Bob-bob-bob
Goes her little round head.
Tame as a pussy-cat
In the street,
Step-step-step
Go her little red feet.
With her little red feet
And her little round head,
Mrs. Peck-Pigeon
Goes picking for bread.

ELEANOR FARJEON

MAN FAT

Man fat
Top hat
Fell flat
Squashed hat.

ANON

JUMP OR JIGGLE

Frogs jump
Caterpillars hump

Worms wiggle
Bugs jiggle

Rabbits hop
Horses clop

Snakes slide
Seagulls glide

Mice creep
Deer leap

Puppies bounce
Kittens pounce

Lions stalk —
But —
I walk!

EVELYN BEYER

HARE SONG

Hare is jumping and singing;
Hare is jumping and singing,
While the wind is roaring,
While the wind is roaring.

Hare is dancing and singing;
Hare is dancing and singing,
While the clouds are roaring,
While the clouds are roaring.

TRADITIONAL NORTH AMERICAN

What a sad sight — dead butterflies
Hanging upon a spider's web.

SHIKI *Japan*

WHISKY FRISKY

Whisky frisky,
Hipperty hop,
Up he goes
To the tree top!

Whirly, twirly,
Round and round,
Down he scampers
To the ground.

Furly, curly,
What a tail,
Tall as a feather,
Broad as a sail.

Where's his supper?
In the shell.
Snappy, cracky,
Out it fell.

ANON

CATS

Cats sleep
Anywhere,
Any table,
Any chair,
Top of piano,
Window-ledge,
In the middle,
On the edge,
Open drawer,
Empty shoe,
Anybody's
Lap will do,
Fitted in a
Cardboard box,
In the cupboard
With your frocks –
Anywhere!
They don't care!
Cats sleep
Anywhere.

ELEANOR FARJEON

THREE MICE

Three little mice walked into town,
Their coats were gray, and their eyes were brown.

Three little mice went down the street,
With woolwork slippers upon their feet.

Three little mice sat down to dine
On curranty bread and gooseberry wine.

Three little mice ate on and on
Till every crumb of the bread was gone.

Three little mice, when the feast was done,
Crept home quietly, one by one.

Three little mice went straight to bed,
And dreamt of crumbly, curranty bread.

CHARLOTTE DRUITT COLE

Jack Sprat's pig,
He was not very little,
Nor yet very big;
He was not very lean,
He was not very fat;
He'll do well for a grunt,
Says little Jack Sprat.

ANON

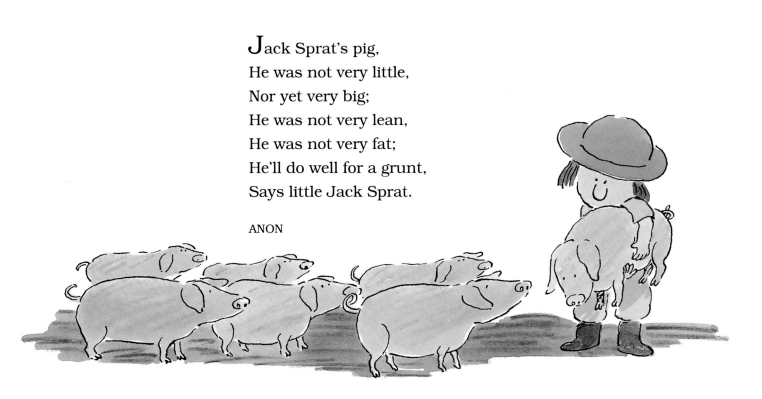

Froggie, froggie.
Hoppity-hop!
When you get to the sea
You do not stop.
Plop!

ANON

THE KANGAROO

Old Jumpety-Bumpety-Hop-and-Go-One
Was lying asleep on his side in the sun.
This old kangaroo, he was whisking the flies
(With his long glossy tail) from his ears and his eyes.
Jumpety-Bumpety-Hop-and-Go-One
Was lying asleep on his side in the sun,
Jumpety-Bumpety-Hop!

TRADITIONAL AUSTRALIAN

JUMBLE JINGLE

Pick up a stick up,
   A stick up now pick;
Let me hear you say that
   Nine times, *quick!*

LAURA E. RICHARDS

22

WHAT ARE YOU?

I am a gold lock;   I am a gold key.

I am a silver lock;   I am a silver key.

I am a brass lock;   I am a brass key.

I am a lead lock;   I am a lead key.

I am a monk lock;   I am a mon —key.

TRADITIONAL CATCH-RHYME

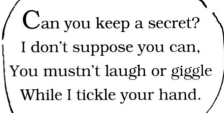

Can you keep a secret?
I don't suppose you can,
You mustn't laugh or giggle
While I tickle your hand.

ANON

OLIVER TWIST

Oliver-Oliver-Oliver Twist
Bet you a penny you can't do this:
Number one — touch your tongue
Number two — touch your shoe
Number three — touch your knee
Number four — touch the floor
Number five — stay alive
Number six — wiggle your hips
Number seven — jump to Heaven
Number eight — bang the gate
Number nine — walk the line
Number ten — start again.

TRADITIONAL

ACKER BACKER

Acker Backer
Soda cracker
Acker Backer four
Acker Backer
Soda cracker
Knock on Acker's door.

TRADITIONAL

UP AND DOWN

Up and down
Up and down
All the way to London Town.
Swish swash
Swish swash
All the way to Charing Cross.
Heel and toe
Heel and toe
All the way to Jericho.

TRADITIONAL

LILY LEE

I like Lily,
Little Lily Lee;
I like Lily
And Lily likes me.
Lily likes lollipops,
Lemonade and lime-drops,
But I like Lily,
Little Lily Lee.

ISOBEL BEST

What's your name?
Mary Jane.
Where do you live?
Down the lane.
What do you keep?
A little shop.
What do you sell?
Ginger pop.
How many bottles do you sell
   in a day?
Twenty-four, now go away.

TRADITIONAL

SO-SO JOE

So-So Joe
de so-so man
wore a so-so suit
with a so-so shoe.
So-So Joe
de so-so man
lived in a so-so house
with a so-so view.
And when you asked
So-So Joe
de so-so man
How do you do?
So-So Joe
de so-so man
would say to you:

*Just so-so
Nothing new.*

JOHN AGARD

Little boy, little boy,
Where'd you get your britches?
Daddy cut 'em out,
And Mama made the stitches.

Leather britches, full of stitches,
Mama sewed the buttons on;
Daddy pushed him out of bed,
Because he had his britches on.

TRADITIONAL

DOCTOR STICKLES

Dr. Stickles tickled me
And I began to giggle
Dr. Stickles tickled harder
Then I began to wiggle
When Dr. Stickles tickled my toes
I laughed and so would you
Then I tickled Dr. Stickles
Because he was ticklish, too!

SHEREE FITCH

HUGH, HUGH

Hugh, Hugh,
At the age of two,
Built his house in a big brown shoe.
Hugh, Hugh,
What'll you do?
There's holes in the soles
And the rain comes through!

DENNIS LEE

Anna Elise, she jumped with surprise;

The surprise was so quick, it played her a trick;

The trick was so rare, she jumped in a chair;

The chair was so frail, she jumped in a pail;

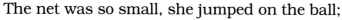

The pail was so wet, she jumped in a net;

The net was so small, she jumped on the ball;

The ball was so round, she jumped on the ground;

And ever since then she's been turning around.

ANON

HONEY BEAR

There was a big bear
Who lived in a cave;
His greatest love
Was honey.
He had twopence a week
Which he never could save,
So he never had
Any money.
I bought him a money box
Red and round,
In which to put
His money.
He saved and saved
Till he got a pound,
Then spent it all
On honey.

ELIZABETH LANG

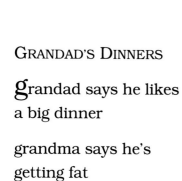

GRANDAD'S DINNERS

grandad says he likes
a big dinner

grandma says he's
getting fat

she tells him he
should try to be thinner

grandad says
"Tell that to the cat!"

JOAN POULSON

KITTY

Look at pretty little Kitty
Gnawing on a bone!
How I wish she'd eat some fish
And leave my leg alone.

DOUG MACLEOD

Happy birthday to you!
Squashed tomatoes and stew;
Eggs and bacon for breakfast,
Happy birthday to you!

ANON

Tippety, tippety tin,
Give me a pancake and I will come in.
Tippety, tippety toe,
Give me a pancake and I will go.

ANON

HOT DOGS FOREVER

Hot dogs for breakfast
Hot dogs for lunch
Hot dogs
Hot dogs
all in a bunch

You can eat 'em with mustard
You can eat 'em with cheese
You can eat 'em
any way you please

Eat 'em from the bar-B-Q
Eat 'em from the pot
Eat 'em cold or
Eat 'em hot
Eat 'em standing up
or down on your knees

Hot dogs
Hot dogs
Please Please Please

SONJA DUNN

ZELBA ZINNAMON

Zelba Zinnamon
She loved cinnamon
She loved cinnamon cake
Zelba Zinnamon
Ate so much cinnamon
She got a belly ache

Then Zelba Zinnamon
Sniffed the cinnamon
Got her nose all red
Zelba Zinnamon
Nose full of cinnamon
Had to go to bed.

SHEREE FITCH

CHOCOLATE MILKSHAKE

Into the blender . . . . .
chocolate
1 spoon 2 spoon 3 spoon
what the heck
4 spoon 5 spoon
now the milk
glug . . . glug . . . slurp
scoop in the ice-cream
plop . . . plop . . .
turn the switch
shake . . . shake . . . slurp . . .
gurgle . . . gurgle . . .
pour into glass
glug . . . glug . . .

Ahh

TANIA MEAD

IF YOU'RE NO GOOD AT COOKING

If you're no good at cooking,
Can't fry or bake,

Here's something you
Can always make. Take

Three very ordinary
Slices of bread:

Stack the second
On the first one's head.

Stack the third
On top of that.

There! Your three slices
Lying pat.

So what have you got?
A BREAD SANDWICH,

That's what!
Why not?

KIT WRIGHT

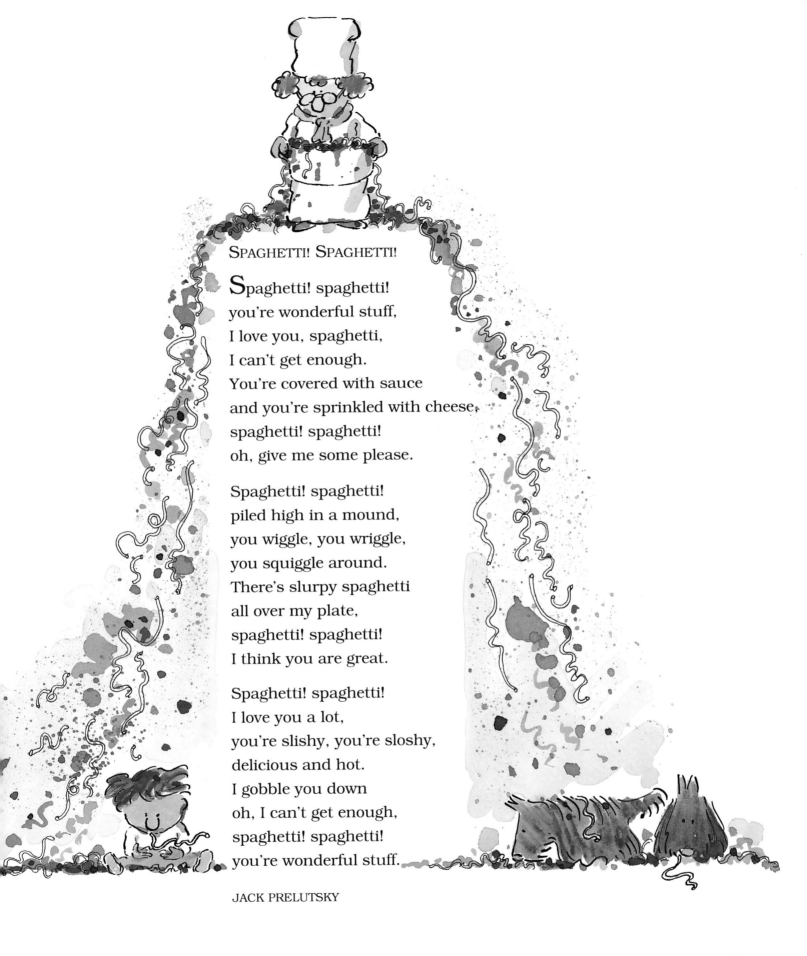

SPAGHETTI! SPAGHETTI!

Spaghetti! spaghetti!
you're wonderful stuff,
I love you, spaghetti,
I can't get enough.
You're covered with sauce
and you're sprinkled with cheese,
spaghetti! spaghetti!
oh, give me some please.

Spaghetti! spaghetti!
piled high in a mound,
you wiggle, you wriggle,
you squiggle around.
There's slurpy spaghetti
all over my plate,
spaghetti! spaghetti!
I think you are great.

Spaghetti! spaghetti!
I love you a lot,
you're slishy, you're sloshy,
delicious and hot.
I gobble you down
oh, I can't get enough,
spaghetti! spaghetti!
you're wonderful stuff.

JACK PRELUTSKY

35

A man said to me,
"Can you sing?"
I said, "Sing?"
He said, "Yes."
I said, "Who?"
He said, "You."
I said, "Me?"
He said, "Yes."
I said, "When?"
He said, "Now."
I said, "Now?"
He said, "Yes."
I said, "No."
He said, "Oh."

ANON

I am running in a circle
and my feet are getting sore,
and my head is
spinning
spinning
as it's never spun before,
I am
dizzy
dizzy
dizzy.
Oh! I cannot bear much more,
I am trapped in a
revolving
. . .volving
. . .volving
. . .volving door!

JACK PRELUTSKY

LITTLE JUMPING JOAN

Here am I,
Little Jumping Joan;
When nobody's with me
I'm all alone.

ANON

MRS. BROWN

Mrs. Brown went to town,
Riding on a pony,
When she came back,
She lost her hat,
And called on Miss Maloney.

ANON *A Scottish variation of* Yankee Doodle

THE RAT CATCHER

I can catch rats and voles!
And anything that lives in holes!
I can catch rats and voles,
Rats and voles and weasels!

TRADITIONAL

DAN, DAN

Dan, Dan, the funny wee man,
Washed his face in the frying pan,
Combed his hair with the leg of the chair,
Dan, Dan, the funny wee man.

ANON

THE SONGSTER

Miss Pauncefort sang at the top of her voice
(Sing tirry-lirry-lirry down the lane)
And nobody knew what she sang about
(Sing tirry-lirry-lirry all the same).

STEVIE SMITH

LITTLE TEE-WEE

Little Tee-Wee,
He went to sea,
In an open boat;
And while afloat,
The little boat bended.
My story's ended.

ANON

BOO HOO

Mabel cried as she stood by the window,
Mabel cried as she stood by the door.
Mabel cried and her tears filled three buckets;
Mabel cried as she sat on the floor.

Mabel cried for oh so many hours,
Mabel cried for oh so many more.
With her tears then she watered her flowers;
With the rest then she mopped up the floor.

ARNOLD SPILKA

MABEL MURPLE

Mabel Murple's house was purple
So was Mabel's hair
Mabel Murple's cat was purple
Purple everywhere.

Mabel Murple's bike was purple
So were Mabel's ears
And when Mabel Murple cried
She cried terrible purple tears.

SHEREE FITCH

BIBBLIBONTY

On the Bibblibonty hill
Stands a Bibblibonty house;
In the Bibblibonty house
Are Bibblibonty people;
The Bibblibonty people
Have Bibblibonty children;
And the Bibblibonty children
Take a Bibblibonty sup
With a Bibblibonty spoon
From a Bibblibonty cup.

ROSE FYLEMAN *from the Dutch*

DE BOTTLEMAN

Bottles! Bottles!
Bottles I buy.
Hear de bottleman cry

Long bottles
Short bottles
Fat bottles
Thin bottles

Bottles! Bottles!
Bottles I buy.
Hear de bottleman cry

Search low search high.
I buy dem wet
I buy dem dry

Run with a bottle
to de bottleman cart
when yuh hear de bottleman cry

Bottles! Bottles!
Bottles I buy

JOHN AGARD

SUGAR TRAIN

Going downhill from Mundoo
For sugar
Making a noise as it climbs the hill
The railway
Going downhill from Mundoo
For sugar
Making a noise as it climbs the hill
The railway
Going downhill from Mundoo
For sugar
Making a noise as it climbs the hill
    aaa, eee, ooo

GEORGE WATSON

PORTRAIT OF A MOTORCAR

It's a lean car . . . a long-legged dog of a car . . . a gray-ghost
  eagle car.
The feet of it eat the dirt of a road . . . the wings of it eat the hills.

CARL SANDBURG

THE HILL WAS STEEP

The hill was steep,
So steep I could not climb it.
I tried and I tried
But I could not do it.
So I came down for a rest.
I think going down is best.

RAJ TANDAY *Age 8*

Freewheeling on a bike —
the butterflies of sunlight
all over me.

ROBERT GRAY

GOODNESS GRACIOUS!

Goodness gracious, fiddle dee dee!
Somebody's grandmother out at sea!

Just where the breakers begin to bound
Somebody's grandmother bobbing around.

Up on the shore the people shout,
"Give us a hand and we'll pull you out!"

"No!" says the granny. "I'm right as rain,
And I'm going to go on till I get to Spain."

MARGARET MAHY

NICHOLAS NAYLOR

Nicholas Naylor
The deep-blue sailor
Sailed the sea
As a master-tailor.

He sewed for the Captain,
He sewed for the crew,
He sewed up the kit-bags
And hammocks too.

He sewed up a serpent,
He sewed up a shark,
He sewed up a sailor
In a bag of dark.

How do you like
Your work, master-tailor?
"So, so, so,"
Said Nicholas Naylor.

CHARLES CAUSLEY

IF YOU EVER

If you ever ever ever ever ever
    If you ever ever ever meet a whale
You must never never never never never
    You must never never never touch its tail:
For if you ever ever ever ever ever
    If you ever ever ever touch its tail,
You will never never never never never
    You will never never meet another whale.

ANON

"Splash," said a raindrop
   As it fell upon my hat;
"Splash," said another
   As it trickled down my back.
"You are very rude," I said
   As I looked up to the sky;
Then *another* raindrop splashed
   Right into my eye!

ANON

APRIL RAIN SONG

Let the rain kiss you.
Let the rain beat upon your head
   with silver liquid drops.
Let the rain sing you a lullaby.

The rain makes still pools on the sidewalk.
The rain makes running pools in the gutter.
The rain plays a little sleep-song
   on our roof at night —

And I love the rain.

LANGSTON HUGHES

RAIN, RAIN

Rain, rain, go away,
Come again another day.

Rain, rain, go away
Don't come back till Christmas day.

Rain, rain, pour down,
But not a drop on our town.

ANON

RINSES IN THE RAIN

I saw a lady with red hair
talking to one with blue on

the sun shone
and the rain ran
the streets emptied
the people had gone

when I looked
for the ladies again
there was a purple stream
flowing down the drain

MICHAEL ROSEN

IN THE RAIN

There is no colour in the rain
It's only water, wet and plain.
It makes damp spots upon my book
And splashes on my new dress, look!
But puddles, in the rainy weather,
Glisten like a peacock's feather.

RENÉ CLOKE

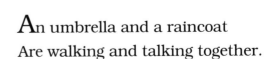

An umbrella and a raincoat
Are walking and talking together.

BUSON *Japan*

51

SAND

Sand in your fingernails
Sand between your toes
Sand in your earholes
Sand up your nose!

Sand in your sandwiches
Sand on your bananas
Sand in your bed at night
Sand in your pyjamas!

Sand in your sandals
Sand in your hair
Sand in your knickers
Sand everywhere!

JOHN FOSTER

SMALL TALK

"Hello, Blue."
"How are you?"
"I'm fine."
"Me too."

"How's Sue?"
"Nothing new."
"How about you?"
"Not much to do."

"What do you say?"
"I'm OK."
"Want to play?"
"Not today."

"Hello, Blue."
"How are you?"
"I'm fine."
"Me, too."

DUNCAN BALL

I CAN'T TAKE THE SUN NO MORE, MAN

I can't take the sun no more, Man.
I buy fifty cans of cola,
I take my clothes off,
But I'm still hot.
I might as well take off my skin
It's so so so so hot, Man.
I just can't take the sun no more.
I might as well take myself apart
Before the sun melts me.
It's so so so so so so so so so so
Hot, Man.
Just can't take the sun, Man.

LINVAL QUINLAND   *Age 10*

Peter's pop kept a lollipop shop,
And the lollipop shop kept Peter.

ANON

Snow Thoughts

What does a snowman eat?
What does a snowman drink?
What does a snowman dream?
What does a snowman think?

JOHN CUNLIFFE

Footprints in the Snow

When the cats make tracks,
there's just one set of tracks . . .

When they jump from the window
they put their feet in the same places.

This proves, as you ought to know,
that cats don't like snow.

GAVIN EWART

I see Dinah Price
Sliding on the ice,
I think slides are nice,
So does Dinah Price.

ANON

The more it snows
　　(Tiddely pom),
The more it goes
　　(Tiddely pom),
The more it goes
　　(Tiddely pom)
　　On snowing.
And nobody knows
　　(Tiddely pom),
How cold my toes
　　(Tiddely pom),
How cold my toes
　　(Tiddely pom),
　　Are growing.

A.A. MILNE

The north wind doth blow,
And we shall have snow,
And what will poor robin do then?
　　Poor thing.
He'll sit in a barn,
And keep himself warm,
And hide his head under his wing.
　　Poor thing.

ANON

THE KITTY RAN UP THE TREE

The kitty ran up the tree,
The kitty ran up the tree,
Her nose went up
And her toes went up
And the kitty ran up the tree.

Why did she climb the tree?
To see what a kitty could see.
But all she could see
At the top of the tree
Was the tip of the top of the tree —

So —

The kitty came down the tree,
The kitty came down the tree,
Her nose came down
And her toes came down
And the kitty came down the tree.

DENNIS LEE

BEETLE

A little beetle passed me by,
He didn't make much fuss,
He ran around my garden
Like a tiny yellow bus.

SYLVIA GERDTZ

MY GERBIL

My gerbil doesn't bite
But if you poke him
then he might . . .

RIK MARTIN

A LITTLE TALK

The big brown hen and Mrs. Duck
Went walking out together;
They talked about all sorts of things —
The farmyard, and the weather.
But all I heard was: "Cluck!
    Cluck! Cluck!"
And "Quack! Quack! Quack!"
    from Mrs. Duck.

ANON

Someone stole the hedgehog
We only knew as "Jack."
I used to trim his toenails
And scratch his little back.

WILBUR G. HOWCROFT

THE DINERS IN THE KITCHEN

Our dog Fred
Et the bread

Our dog Dash
Et the hash

Our dog Pete
Et the meat

Our dog Davy
Et the gravy

Our dog Toffy
Et the coffee

And — the worst
From the first —

Our dog Fido
Et the pie-dough.

JAMES WHITCOMB RILEY

58

MY PUPPY

It's funny
my puppy
knows just how I feel.

When I'm happy
he's yappy
and squirms like an eel.

When I'm grumpy
he's slumpy
and stays at my heel.

It's funny
my puppy
knows such a great deal.

AILEEN FISHER

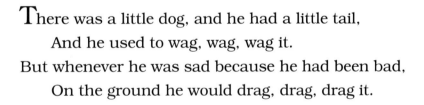

There was a little dog, and he had a little tail,
    And he used to wag, wag, wag it.
But whenever he was sad because he had been bad,
    On the ground he would drag, drag, drag it.

He had a little nose, as of course you would suppose,
    And on it was a muz-muz-muzzle,
And to get it off he'd try till a tear stood in his eye,
    But he found it a puz-puz-puzzle.

ANON

PING-PONG

Chitchat
wigwag
rickrack
zigzag

knickknack
gewgaw
riffraff
seesaw

crisscross
flip-flop
ding-dong
tiptop

singsong
mishmash
King Kong
   bong.

EVE MERRIAM

I Won't

I won't, no I won't, no I won't do that.
I don't want to, I don't have to,
No I won't wear that hat.

I hate it, yes I hate it, yes I hate hate hate.
You can't make me, I don't want to,
I don't care if we are late.

Yes I'm naughty, yes I'm naughty,
Yes I know, know, know.
But I won't wear that hat
So it's No! No! No!

MICHELLE MAGORIAN

PIGGY TO JOEY

Piggy to Joey,
Piggy to Joe,
Yes, that's what I was —
Piggy to Joe.

Will he come back again?
Oh no, no, no.
Oh how I wish I hadn't been
Piggy to Joe.

STEVIE SMITH

I HAVE NONE

Robert has a baby sister
Kay has a baby sister
Kimani and Ayo both have
baby brothers
Janice and Sita have big brothers
and Justin's got a big sister.

All the kids have brothers and sisters
but I have none.

AFUA COOPER

IN THE GARDEN

Went to the garden
Picked up a pin
Asked who was out
Asked who was in.
Nobody in
Nobody out
Down in the garden
Walking about.

ANON

TODAY I SAW A LITTLE WORM

Today I saw a little worm
Wriggling on his belly.
Perhaps he'd like to come inside
And see what's on the Telly.

SPIKE MILLIGAN

MARY MAC

Mary Mac, me shirt is black
What'll I wear on Sunday?
Go to bed and cover me head
And not get up till Monday.

ANON

A GOOD PLAY

We built a ship upon the stairs
All made of the back-bedroom chairs,
And filled it full of sofa pillows
To go a-sailing on the billows.

We took a saw and several nails,
And water in the nursery pails;
And Tom said, "Let us also take
An apple and a slice of cake;" —
Which was enough for Tom and me
To go a-sailing on, till tea.

We sailed along for days and days,
And had the very best of plays;
But Tom fell out and hurt his knee,
So there was no one left but me.

ROBERT LOUIS STEVENSON

VISITING

The little boy next door
At number 74
Has got a top
That doesn't stop —
That's what I go to number seventy-four for.

The people who are new
At number 72
Have lots of toys
For little boys,
So I often go to number seventy-two too.

JONATHAN ALWAYS

I LOVE MY BELT

Plastic belt
Elastic belt
Stretch – stretch – stretch
FANTASTIC belt.

JASMINE LEHAL *Age 5*

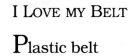

A MOM CALLS FOR HER CHILDREN

Children! Children!
Yes, mom
Where are you?
We are in the forest mom
Come back home
We are afraid
What are you afraid of
A big tiger mom
Where is it?
It's next to the big tree
What is it doing?
It's looking at us
Come, run home.

ALEXANDER MTHOMBENI *Africa*

FAIRY STORY

I went into the wood one day
And there I walked and lost my way

When it was so dark I could not see
A little creature came to me

He said if I would sing a song
The time would not be very long

But first I must let him hold my hand tight
Or else the wood would give me a fright

I sang a song, he let me go
But now I am home again there is nobody I know.

STEVIE SMITH

Whipper-snapper, rooty-tooty,
Helter-skelter, tutti-frutti;
Have a wing-ding, silly Billy,
Lickety-split, don't shally-shilly,
Niminy-piminy, willy-nilly,
Hocus-pocus, there's a dear.

Hippety-hoppety, hurry-scurry,
Mumbo-jumbo, don't you worry;
Hurdy-gurdy plays by ear.
Pop's a jim-jam fuddy-duddy,
Namby-pamby is dear muddy;
Pop's a hunky-dory foola,
Muddy, she does hula-hula . . .
Be an eager-beaver, Beulah.

WILLARD R. ESPY

ME AND MY GRANNIE

Me and my Grannie,
And a great lot mair,
Kicked up a row
Going home from the fair.

By came the watchman,
And cried, "Who's there?"
"Me and my Grannie
And a great lot mair."

TRADITIONAL SCOTTISH

AFTER A BATH

After my bath
I try, try, try
to wipe myself
till I'm dry, dry, dry.

Hands to wipe
and fingers and toes
and two wet legs
and a shiny nose.

Just think how much
less time I'd take
if I were a dog
and could shake, shake, shake.

AILEEN FISHER

THE MOON

The moon out
There.
The sun out
There.
The world out
There.
The whole galaxy out
There
and me stuck in my bedroom.

KI ELLWOOD-FRIERY *Age 8*

SILVERLY

Silverly,
    Silverly,
Over the
    Trees
The moon drifts
    By on a
Runaway
    Breeze.

Dozily,
    Dozily,
Deep in her
    Bed,
A little girl
    Dreams with the
Moon in her
    Head.

DENNIS LEE

LATE LAST NIGHT

Late last night
I lay in bed
driving buses
in my head.

MICHAEL ROSEN

THE FALLING STAR

I saw a star slide down the sky,
Blinding the north as it went by,
Too burning and too quick to hold,
Too lovely to be bought or sold,
Good only to make wishes on
And then forever to be gone.

SARA TEASDALE

SONG

Brighter, brighter, shine you moon;
   brighter, brighter, shine you moon.
I will follow the trail to the hot lands;
   I will follow the trail to the hot lands.
Rocks, rocks to step on; rocks, rocks to step on.
Bamboo, bamboo to hold to; bamboo, bamboo to hold to.

TRADITIONAL PHILIPPINES

INDEX OF TITLES AND FIRST LINES

Titles are in *italics*. Where the title and the first line are the same,
the first line only is listed.

U, V

W

Z

INDEX OF POETS

ACKNOWLEDGMENTS

The publisher would like to thank the copyright holders for permission to reproduce the following copyright material:

John Agard: "De Bottleman" and "So-So Joe" from *No Hickory, No Dickory, No Dock* by John Agard and Grace Nichols (Viking, 1991) reprinted by permission of the author c/o Caroline Sheldon. Jonathan Always: "Visiting" from *Light and Humorous Verse* reprinted by permission of Herbert Joseph Ltd. Duncan Ball: "Small Talk" reprinted by permission of the author and New South Wales Department of Education. Evelyn Beyer: "Jump or Jiggle" from *Another Here and Now Story Book* reprinted by permission of Dutton Children's Books, Penguin USA © 1937 by E.P. Dutton, renewed © 1965 by Lucy Sprague Mitchell. Tony Bradman: "I Can Put My Socks On" from *A Kiss on the Nose* (1984) reprinted by permission of Willam Heinemann Ltd. Charles Causley: "Nicholas Naylor" from *Early in the Morning* by Charles Causley © Charles Causley 1986, reprinted by permission of David Higham Associates. René Cloke: "In the Rain" from *A Posy of Little Verses* reprinted by permission of the Hamlyn Publishing Group. Afua Cooper: "I Have None" from *The Red Caterpillar on College Street* © Afua Cooper 1989, reprinted by permission of Sister Vision Press, Toronto. John Cunliffe: "Snow Thoughts" from *Standing on a Strawberry* (Andre Deutsch) reprinted by permission of Scholastic Publications Ltd. Charlotte Druitt Cole: "Three Mice" reprinted by permission of HarperCollins Publishers. Sonja Dunn: "Hot Dogs Forever" from *Butterscotch Dreams* by Sonja Dunn © 1987 by Sonja Dunn, reprinted by permission of Pembroke Publishers Ltd. Ki Ellwood-Friery: "The Moon" from *Cadbury's 9th Book of Children's Poetry* reprinted by permission of the National Exhibition of Children's Art. Willard Espy: "Whipper snapper, rooty-tooty..." from *The Game of Words* by Willard Espy reprinted by permission of Bramhall House. Gavin Ewart: "Footprints in the Snow" from *Like It or Not* by Gavin Ewart (Bodley Head) reprinted by permission of Random House. Eleanor Farjeon: "Cats" from *The Children's Bells* by Eleanor Farjeon and "Mrs Peck-Pigeon" from *Invitation to a Mouse and Other Poems* edited by Annabel Farjeon reprinted by permission of David Higham Associates, © Executors of the estate of Eleanor Farjeon 1916, 1918, 1923, 1928, 1933, 1936, 1938, 1949, 1950, 1951. Max Fatchen: "Hair" from *Songs for my Dog* by Max Fatchen (Penguin) reprinted by permission of John Johnson Ltd. Aileen Fisher: "My Puppy" and "After a Bath" from *Up the Windy Hill* © Aileen Fisher (Abelard Schuman) reprinted by permission of the author. Sheree Fitch: "Doctor Stickles", "Mabel Murple" and "Zelba Zinnamon" from *Toes in my Nose* by Sheree Fitch (1987) reprinted by permission of Doubleday Canada. John Foster: "Sand" from *Four O'Clock Friday* by John Foster (1991) reprinted by permission of O.U.P. Rose Fyleman: "Bibblibonty" from *Widdy-Widdy-Wurkey* reprinted by permission of Blackwells. Sylvia Gerdtz: "Beetle" from *Big Dipper Rides Again* ed. Epstein, Factor, McKay & Richards (OUP Australia) reprinted by permission of O.U.P. Robert Gray: "Freewheeling on a Bike" from *27 Poems* by Robert Gray reprinted by permission of the University of Queensland Press. Wilbur G. Howcroft: "Someone stole the hedgehog..." from *Nonsery Rhymes* © Wilbur G. Howcroft, reprinted by permission of the Hawthorn Press. Langston Hughes: "April Rain Song" from *The Dream Keeper* by Langston Hughes, copyright 1932 by Alfred A. Knopf, Inc. and renewed 1960 by Langston Hughes. Reprinted by permission of the publisher. W. Kingdon-Ward: "Buttons" from *Speech Rhymes* reprinted by permission of A & C Black (Publishers) Ltd. Elizabeth Lang: "Honey Bear" reprinted by permission of HarperCollins Publishers. Dennis Lee: "Hugh, Hugh', "Silverly" and "The Kitty Ran Up the Tree" from *Jelly Belly* (Blackie, 1983) reprinted by permission of

MGA, U.S.A. Jasmine Lehal: "I Love My Belt" from *Cadbury's 9th Book of Children's Poetry* reprinted by permission of the National Exhibition of Children's Art. M. Long: "The Window Cleaner" from *The Book of a Thousand Poems* (Evans Bros) reprinted by permission of HarperCollins Publishers. Doug MacLeod: "Kitty" from *The Fed Up Family Album* by Doug MacLeod reprinted by permission of Penguin Books (Australia) Ltd. Michelle Magorian: "I Won't" from *Waiting for My Shorts to Dry* © Michelle Magorian 1989, reprinted by permission of Rogers, Coleridge & White Ltd. Margaret Mahy: "Goodness Gracious" from *The First Margaret Mahy Story Book* © Margaret Mahy 1972, 1973, 1975, reprinted by permission of J.M. Dent & Sons Ltd. Rik Martin: "My Gerbil" from *One for You, Two for Me* by Rik Martin, reprinted by permission of the author. Tania Mead: "Chocolate Milkshake" from *Take a Chance: An Anthology of Performance Poetry* reprinted by permission of the Australian Association of Teachers. Eve Merriam: "Ping-Pong" © Eve Merriam 1964, 1970, 1973, reprinted by permission of Marian Reiner. Spike Milligan: "Today I Saw a Little Worm" © Spike Milligan 1959, 1961, 1963, reprinted by permission of the author. A.A. Milne: "The More it Snows" from *The House at Pooh Corner* reprinted by permission of Methuen Children's Books. Alexander Mthombeni: "A Mom Calls for her Children" from *The Return of the Amasi Bird* reprinted by permission of Ravan Press, S.A. Grace Nichols: "Sugarcake Bubble" from *No Hickory, No Dickory, No Dock* by John Agard and Grace Nichols (Viking, 1991) reprinted by permission of Curtis Brown Ltd. Joan Poulson: "Grandad's Dinners" from *The Bee's Knees* © Joan Poulson 1990, reprinted by permission of Stride Publishing Co. Jack Prelutsky: "I Am Running in a Circle" from *The New Kid on the Block* reprinted by permission of William Heinemann Ltd. and "Spaghetti! Spaghetti!" from *Rainy Rainy Saturday* © Jack Prelutsky 1980, reprinted by permission of Greenwillow Books, a division of William Morrow & Co Inc. Linval Quinland: "I Can't Take the Sun No More, Man" reprinted by permission of the author and Grasmere School. Laura E. Richards: "Jumble Jingle" from *Tirra Lirra: Rhymes Old and New* © Laura E. Richards 1932, reprinted by permission of Little, Brown & Co. Michael Rosen: "Late Last Night" and "Rinses in the Rain" from *Mind Your Own Business* (Andre Deutsch) reprinted by permission of Scholastic Publications Ltd. Carl Sandburg: "Portrait of a Motorcar" from *Complete Poems of Carl Sandburg* reprinted by permission of Harcourt, Brace, Jovanovich Inc. Clive Sansom: "The Dustman" from *Speech Rhymes* by Clive Sansom reprinted by permission of A & C Black (Publishers) Ltd. Stevie Smith: "Fairy Story', "Piggy to Joey" and "The Songster" from *The Collected Poems of Stevie Smith* reprinted by permission of New Directions Publishing Corporation. Arnold Spilka: "Boo-Hoo" from *A Lion I Can Do Without* by Arnold Spilka, reprinted by permission of Marian Reiner. Raj Tanday: "The Hill Was Steep" from *Cadbury's 8th Book of Children's Poetry* reprinted by permission of the National Exhibition of Children's Art. Sara Teasdale: "The Falling Star" from *Collected Poems by Sara Teasdale* © Sara Teasdale 1930, renewed 1958 by Guarantee Trust Co. of NY Executor, reprinted by permission of Macmillan Publishing Co. Charles Thomson: "Up to the Ceiling" © Charles Thomson 1990 from *Mr Mop Has a Floppy Top* (Stanford Books) reprinted by permission of the author. George Watson: "Sugar Train" from *The Honey-Ant Men's Love Song* reprinted by permission of the University of Queensland Press. Kit Wright: "If You're No Good at Cooking" from *Rabbiting On and Other Poems* reprinted by permission of HarperCollins Publishers.

More Kingfisher Paperbacks to Enjoy

THE KINGFISHER NURSERY RHYME SONGBOOK
Selected by Sally Emerson
Illustrated by Colin and Moira Maclean

THE KINGFISHER PLAYTIME TREASURY
Edited by Pie Corbett
Illustrated by Colin and Moira Maclean

THE KINGFISHER BOOK OF CHILDREN'S POETRY
Selected Michael Rosen
Illustrated by Alice Englander

WALKING ON THE BRIDGE OF YOUR NOSE
Selected by Michael Rosen
Illustrated by Chloe Cheese